LEARNINGS FROM
1,000
TEESPRING
CAMPAIGNS

From a 6 Figure Marketer

AFFENGINEER.COM

LEARNINGS FROM 1,000 TEESPRING CAMPAIGNS

From A 6 Figure Marketer

Written By: Mateen Soudagar

More Teespring Tutorial Videos and Guides @ www.Affengineer.com

Learnings From 1,000 Teespring Campaigns
Copyright © 2015 by AffEngineer

Table Of Contents

Background - About Me

Firstly, I'd like to say thank you to everyone that downloaded this book!

I'm just a regular guy like you who is very stubborn in everything he does. If someone out there is making a million dollars doing a certain something, then I'll try the same thing till it starts to make me a million too. No matter how long it takes.

Teespring was my first such stubborn adventure. After reading plenty of success stories on forums and online in general, I decided to give it a shot.

50 campaigns later, I had my first successful campaign and a whole year later, I made 6 figures in pure profit.

I have documented my journey, including monthly financial reports on my blog, affengineer.com.

I urge you all to go through the Teespring tutorial videos on the blog, especially if you're serious about this.

Ok..Let's get started!

Success Comes With Persistence

There's not a single thing I've had success with unless I've stuck to it consistently for a long period of time.

Many people have a rush of motivation on the first day they learn about Teespring. The second day, it will still be there. On the 3rd and 4th day, it will start to die down and a fortnight later, you probably would have given up without even trying.

This is the nature of the human being. They thrive on excitement and this is totally normal.

Teespring, or business in general requires you to be persistent and at a certain stage overcome this thinking approach.

It took me 50 campaigns to find my first profitable campaign. Yes, 50! At the start I was really motivated but after 20 campaigns of nothing, I had to force myself to continue.

As long as you are learning, you're doing things right so you should continue.

It probably won't take that long for you, due to how much information is now available on the internet about Teespring but it paints a picture of reality.

Don't stop after 1 or 2 campaign launches. Have a simple goal. Something like, ' find a pro fitable campaign'. 'Or have 1 day of being in pro fit'.

Stick to it till you achieve it.

Teespring is NOT a Passive Business

I'm sure many of us are trying to crack the online business code hoping it will give us the time to do whatever we want.

We'd like to some day have a business earning us $xxx/day while we spend the whole day immersed in our hobbies and doing the things we really love.

There definitely are some businesses like that *but* Teespring is not one of them.

I'd spend 4-6 hours launching designs every day. I'd aim for 10-15 different designs. Then I'd have to monitor them during the day and maybe even launch more designs as some show hints of success.

Even if I had a 1k profit/day campaign, I'd STILL have to do the above. Why? Well, what's going to happen 2 weeks after my campaign dies to $0/day? I need something to replace it right?

Teespring campaigns are short lived. Even if you find something big, it will last a few weeks MAX and will die out. You'll be on the hunt to find another one.

If you want to do this Full-Time, you need to know the volatility of the business.

Teespring isn't Saturated, it's Just Harder

'Business saturation' is an excuse to not try. Never say something is saturated because it isn't. There is ALWAYS opportunity to turn a profit somewhere.

I've monitored niches for months thinking that theres just no way someone can launch a pro fitable campaign in this niche anymore because of how many campaigns I've seen launched in it.

2 weeks later, I'd see a 1,000+ campaign in that exact niche. People will still buy things if they like them enough.

It will de finitely get harder though and you're not going to trun a pro fit if you do the same thing everyone else is doing.

Each campaign I've seen sell well these days, has been something unique and refreshing. Something that can be proudly shared on someones wall knowing that none of their friends have seen it yet.

Work Harder Than Others

This is connected to the above point.

I've seen so many people come in, find a campaign that sold well previously and copy the exact same words with a slightly different design and try sell it again.

Why the heck do you think that will work? It's obviously been marketed to the same demographic you're targeting. These people have *already* made up their mind on whether they want to buy the design or not, then someone else comes along showing them the *same* thing.

You can't do this, it doesn't work. You need to design well, market better, use your creativity a little bit to come up with something wearable.

If you won't buy your design, chances are no one else will.

Remember, it's not just about making sales. You need to make enough sales that it's outweighing your advertising costs and to do this, you need to have a great design.

I remained pro fitable for 12 consecutive months because I worked harder than most people. I focused on launching 10-15 campaigns a day because I knew most people would think it was impossible.

Basic Photoshop Skills are a HUGE Advantage

So many people want to get into Teespring and outsource everything straight away. I'm sure Tim Ferris's '4 Hour Work Week' had something to do with this thinking.

There's nothing wrong with outsourcing, but remember that it takes time to go back and forth with your designer till you get things right.

Creativity is tough to explain over a Skype chat or via email so there will de finitely be some disconnect there.

Due to time differences, I'd sometimes have to wait 48 hours till my designer gave me something I was happy to use. In this 48 hours someone could have launched the same design I wanted and gone through my demographic. It's happened before.

Photoshop may be new to you but it is one of THE best skills an online entrepreneur can learn. It's not hard, and a few weekends of practice will get you very far.

I have a Teespring Design Course on my blog which goes through over 20 videos of Photoshop techniques I've used on my campaigns. I can't think of one thing I haven't covered in that course. De finitely check it out.

Pockets of Gold Mines are EVERYWHERE

If you go through my monthly reports, you'll notice there are a few times I'll hit red, then I'll hit a long streak of green again because I've found a design(s) that works.

This happens all the time. There are pockets of $$ EVERYWHERE, you just have to persevere enough to find them. The only way I've been able to do this is by focusing mainly on launching more campaigns at in many niches/sub-niches I can find.

You may not find it in the first 5 campaigns campaigns you launch but just keep going.

Imagine a big grass field where everyone is digging for gold. There gold nuggets everywhere, some have been found, some still exist. You're one of those miners looking for a pocket of gold.

Teespring is Not as easy as People Make it Seem

When you find something that works, it will be a money making machine for a few weeks and life will be simple and sweet but the journey to get to that point is not easy.

Many people try Teespring completely underestimating the amount of effort required. It's hard enough to cross all the hurdles required to learn everything but then you have to keep following the process again and again, till you find something that works.

Although it's tough, I encourage it for everyone because it teaches you how real business works. It's full effort with high rewards.

It WILL get easier as you become more adept at the process but perseverance is needed to get to that point and unless you have that type of attitude, you'll just be one of the many 1000's of people that gave up. Don't be that person!

Most Important FaceBook Data

If you're completely new to FaceBook advertising than the below points may not make sense to you.

People get too analytical sometimes but for the most part of Teespring the below items are what you need to monitor to make a decision on your campaign.

Comments: What are people saying about your design on FaceBook? Do they like it, dislike it? Are they suggesting something else? Are you getting messages asking for a variation of your shirt? Are other people hating on it because they support another view, (might be another good niche!).

CTR: (Click Through Rate). I've gone through this countless times. After doing this for a while you start seeing a pattern between CTR & sales. There's a lot the CTR can tell you. The audience might give you a big CTR because they're passionate but won't buy because they've been sold 10s of shirts. This tells you the audience is either not a buyer demographic or have been sold to numerous times before. Usually it's the latter.

Cost vs Revenue, (Sales)

An obvious one. Once I start seeing my ROI is above 100% I'll start to increase the budget. A lot of newbies will continue to spend hoping somehow sales will pick up. If you've spent $25 or so on your shirt and no sales, just cut it and make another design.

I'm sure there's more, but I've gone through it all in my TS Tutorials section.

There is Money in Sub-Niches

There is money in sub-niches. For example, a shirt directed at a particular rugby team is more likely to give you a positive ROI then one made for rugby fans in general. Why? Because chances are no ones made a shirt JUST for them yet. Think of how many sub-niches there are, literally 100s of thousands.

Another example is making a shirt for Siamese cats instead of cats in general. You get the idea? The more you can appeal to the person/demographic that will see your shirt, the better chance you have of selling it.

There is money in New Design Concepts

Sure, you might be able to make money in broad niches like rugby. But your design has to be fresh/new and REALLY good. If you take the Nurse niche for example. These guys have been sold to SO many times, they've become blind to TeeSpring ads on their FB Newsfeed.

You have to come up with something amazing to get them to pull out their credit card **again** and make a purchase. You can make money in this for sure, just don't do the same thing that everyone else is doing.

Teespring is a Numbers Game

Many newbies start off launching 1 campaign and will focus on JUST that. Although this may seem like a good strategy when you're starting off, once you get faster start to launch 3-5 TS Campaigns at a time and see what data you get back.

The more products you have out there, the faster you'll learn about which niches are hot and what demographics convert better than others. Basically, you're knowledge progression will be much quicker.

Once something shows signs of profitability, THEN you start to focus on it and cut out the losers.

Targeting the Most Passionate First

I don't think many people do this. When targeting interests on FB, I always add about 15-20,000 of the MOST passionate people I can find on FB for that particular niche. There's no point adding 700k-1Mil audience when you're test budget will only reach about 10,000 of them. Do the bare minimum to **test.** The easier you make the process, the less frustrated you'll get.

For example, if I've made a shirt for the horse niche, I'll add a couple of horse magazines and state-wide associations. That should be enough. Once I see I'm profiting, then I add a bunch of more highly targeted interests. Once even this starts to saturate, (frequency increases above 1.5), I'll add all more horse related interests, ones that aren't THAT targeted but might have an audience that will buy.

At the start though, just target enough of an audience so your $10-$25 test ad spend will get to the most targeted audience you can possibly find. If these guys don't buy, no one will.

Knowledge is KEY

You want to keep updated on the latest updates Teespring makes to their platform so you can get in before anyone else. For example, a while ago Teespring released kids apparel.

If you had gotten on it early I'm sure you'd have stumbled upon opportunities others haven't seen yet. Some good communities are Teespring University, Teespring Mastermind and Aff Playbook Paid Forums. Aff Playbook have shared a lot of tips and tricks that have been directly responsible for pretty much ALL my Teespring income, (not exaggerating).

Simplify the whole Process

When I first started Teespring I'd set up a niche FB page, write a custom description, set a different set of colors, etc, for EACH design. Needless to say I'd launch a campaign every hour. Now, I'll launch 2, sometimes even 15 campaigns in an hour. I use ONE facebook group, ONE description template, ONE color/product set.

You get the idea? Make it robotic, something you barely have to think about. The more unnecessary stuff you can cut out, the better. Once a campaign/design picks up and starts bringing in decent sales, you can always fine tune things and make a dedicated FB page for it. For now, make the system/process simple or you'll get sick of it and stop.

Your Designs Need to be Quality

When I first started, my designs were SO bad. I'd slap on some text without worrying about the font or size or even placement, and expect to see results. I'm not saying text designs don't work in-fact the majority of best-sellers have been text based designs.

I'm saying, take at-least SOME time to make your design wearable. Whether it's adjusting the text size and placement so it's in a nice, wearable position, or adding a designers touch to the text by chosing an adequate font for the niche/gender, rotating it, adding a border, blending it into some other text, etc. Over time, you'll get good at this.

Get Rid of your Perfectionist Mentality

This is what kills it for many people in business.

I see WAY to many people that spend too much time on their first design. Analysing why it didn't work, making a re-design of it etc. I make at least 5 designs at a time. As soon as my $30 spend results in no sales, I'll scrap it and move on to another design.

It's better to make another design than to spend countless hours on the same one. Teespring is a quantities game.

Those that are successful have launched 100's if not thousands of designs. I, myself have launched over 1,800 designs/variations. It took me 50 campaigns to even get one to tip! Just keep launching campaigns and you'll learn a tonne about which designs/niches/countries convert.

Keeping an Eye on Working Designs

Research is a MASSIVE part of the process. Most people that get started with Teespring just brain storm some ideas and get designing. This MIGHT work, but chances are it won't.

Monitor pages that continuously launch designs. Every now and then you'll see winning designs. These can be used as inspiration to unlock niches you haven't tried and quotes/sayings that work well. Add your own spin to it and launch designs. Lots of them. I've found heaps of 1,000+ campaigns this way which you'll never find off basic teespring.com/discover or teeview.

Teespring Experience is Very Transferable

Apart from the money, the most valuable thing I've gained during this adventure is the process required to be successful in business.

From the right marketing to whipping up a design in minutes, I've been able to transfer the same model to build lists in the 10s of thousands in weeks.

Whatever you decide to do online, whether it's Teespring or something else, just know that the skills learnt are completely transferrable and will add to your success ratio in anything you do.

That's why many people advise to stick to one thing till it works. Reason being, once you make it work, chanced are you've already gained 50%+ of the knowledge required to make the next thing work.

Use it as a ground to learn core business principals, whatever you decide to do from then on is completely up to you.

Ending Remarks

There are some things that take a while to get good at. Teespring is one of them. If you're serious about this business don't be naive and think success will come with your first campaign. Be ready for a rough path but one that has rewards in place for those that percivier enough.

How else will the business universe decide who's worthy of the rewards it has in place? With every hurdle you cross, you'll be one step ahead of those that gave up at that point.

Whether it's Teespring or some other business venture you embark on in the near future, just remember to be a little headstrong about it. Get to work and work hard. Nothing comes without grinding it out.

If you're prepared for this, you're on your way to succeed.

Did you like this eBook?

Give it a review on Amazon and let me know your thoughts!

If it's crap, let me know, if it's good let me know, I strive to produce quality contents for my readers and hope this has been up to your standard.

All the best.

- Mateen @ Affengineer.com